OF ENTIRETY SAY THE SENTENCE

WAVE BOOKS / SEATTLE AND NEW YORK

ERNST MEISTER
OF ENTIRETY SAY THE SENTENCE

///

TRANSLATED BY GRAHAM FOUST AND SAMUEL FREDERICK

PUBLISHED BY WAVE BOOKS

WWW.WAVEPOETRY.COM

SAGE VOM GANZEN DEN SATZ COPYRIGHT © 1972 RIMBAUD

VERLAGSGESELLSCHAFT MBH, AACHEN, GERMANY

ENGLISH TRANSLATION AND INTRODUCTION

COPYRIGHT © 2015 BY GRAHAM FOUST AND SAMUEL FREDERICK

ALL RIGHTS RESERVED

WAVE BOOKS TITLES ARE DISTRIBUTED TO THE TRADE BY

CONSORTIUM BOOK SALES AND DISTRIBUTION

PHONE: 800-283-3572 / SAN 631-760X

LIBRARY OF CONGRESS CATALOGING-IN-PUBLICATION DATA

MEISTER, ERNST, 1911–1979.

[SAGE VOM GANZEN DEN SATZ. ENGLISH]

OF ENTIRETY SAY THE SENTENCE / ERNST MEISTER ; TRANSLATED

BY GRAHAM FOUST AND SAMUEL FREDERICK. — FIRST EDITION.

PAGES CM

ISBN 978-1-940696-16-4 (LIMITED EDITION HARDCOVER)

ISBN 978-1-940696-17-1 (TRADE PBK.)

I. FOUST, GRAHAM W., 1970– TRANSLATOR.

II. FREDERICK, SAMUEL, TRANSLATOR. III. TITLE.

PT2625.E3224S313 2015

831'.914—DC23

2014045434

DESIGNED AND COMPOSED BY QUEMADURA

PRINTED IN THE UNITED STATES OF AMERICA

9 8 7 6 5 4 3 2 1

FIRST EDITION

INTRODUCTION

Sage vom Ganzen den Satz (*Of Entirety Say the Sentence*) is the first volume of an informal trilogy comprising Ernst Meister's final three books; it is followed by *Im Zeitspalt* (*In Time's Rift*) and *Wandloser Raum* (*Wallless Space*). While we can't provide notes as thorough and wide-ranging as those available in the German-language critical edition of Meister's poems (*Gedichte: Textkritische und kommentierte Ausgabe*, published by Wallstein Verlag in 2011), we hope that this introduction will illuminate some of Meister's major concerns during the composition of the poems herein, particularly two events—one an anniversary, the other a tragedy—that occurred in 1970. Of the book's composition, Meister says:

> I understand [1970] as a peculiar year; I was even for a time tempted to choose "Peculiar Year" as its title. This would obviously have indicated something too personal. All in all no thought about what happened during this year remained. In fact, circumstances coincided whose principal significance would have demanded the most alert consideration.
>
> The subjunctive was at that time an indicative for me—I understood something. There was a dead man

whose 200th birthday was being remembered with celebrations and writings, and there was a dead man from recent times with a swarm of obituaries. —In short, 127 years ago Hölderlin met his maker, and Celan had gone into the Seine.

Indeed, numerous poems in this book contain allusions (often oblique ones) to the lives and works of these two German-language writers. In "Demnach, nach-" (on page 22) Meister even brings them together by playing on Celan's "Tübingen, Jänner," a poem that quotes Hölderlin's hymn "Der Rhein." Celan's poem begins, in John Felstiner's translation, as follows:

> Eyes talked in-
> to blindness.
> Their—"a
> riddle, what is pure-
> ly arisen"—, their
> memory of
> floating Hölderlintowers, gull-
> enswirled.

and, after asserting that a man speaking of "this time" could merely "babble," ends with the parenthetical final line,

> ("Pallaksch. Pallaksch.")

In the notes to his translation, Felstiner remarks that "Pallaksch" is a word Hölderlin "was given to uttering in his dementia . . . [a word] that could signify Yes or No," and we see that in Meister's poem Hölderlin's stammering is transposed to the river—Hölderlin lived the second half of his life in a tower on the Neckar River, a tributary of the Rhine—while the pure arisen-ness ("Rein- / entsprungenes"—note the pun) of the riddle is transferred to the animal in the forest who bounds past ("sprang") as it tracks its own scent. Meister picks up the sentence that follows the words Celan quotes from "Der Rhein" ("Even / The song may hardly reveal it") late in *Of Entirety* in the poem that begins "Killed / by his own hand" (on page 153)—no doubt a reference to Celan—and ends:

> No one will grasp
> this soluble thing,
> unless he were to understand
> the whole ruse.
>
> This is a song.

Meister's song echoes Celan's song, which in turn echoes Hölderlin's song, and indeed the word "song" (*Lied* in the German) appears throughout this book, perhaps most notably in the first line of the poem that follows the one above, as well as in the lines "Der Mensch / hat sein Lied zu singen," which appear both in the book's proem and in the poem that begins "Der neben mir" (on page 84). *Lied* is an anagram of *Leid* (meaning "sorrow" or "suffering"); thus the two words contain one another, so that what's sorrowful "echoes back"—to quote from the poem beginning "Wenn wir" (on page 6)—in what's "singable." *Of Entirety Say the Sentence* is Meister's most self-reflexive and tradition-laden exploration of poetry's abilities to sound out the space in which these echoes —psalmic and plaintive—reverberate, and sometimes fade away.

As we note in our introductions to *In Time's Rift* and *Wall-less Space*, Meister never found favor with German literary institutions such as the Gruppe 47, and one reason for this was likely his lack of direct engagement (in either his poems or his public statements) with Germany's Nazi past. Unlike his contemporary Günter Eich, whose poems written as a prisoner of war established his postwar reputation, Meister's verse does not reflect on his time as a soldier or as a prisoner, nor does it confront the horrors of the concentration camps, as Celan most famously does in his poem "Death Fugue." In fact, Meister seems to eschew concrete historical settings altogether in his late verse, forging abstract spaces for metaphysical reflection that may be occasioned by but is never fully bound to actual events. And yet, strangely, particularly because Meister keeps returning to Celan's suicide in poem after poem, the subject of Nazi atrocities appears faintly visible behind some of this volume's phrases and images.

We would like to draw attention to one poem that we believe could be read as Meister's only work that directly deals with Auschwitz. Our reading hinges on a marginal note to one of the notebook versions of the poem "Pünktlich gehts zu"

("Things happen punctually"—page 95). Next to the second stanza of one draft, Meister has written, "When *was* that at Wansee." Although he misspells the word, Meister seems to be thinking of the Berlin suburb of Wannsee, where, on January 20, 1942, high-ranking Nazi officials met in a villa to discuss and implement the en masse killing of Jews, calling this "the final solution to the Jewish question." With this historical event in mind the poem opens up to a new reading in which one of Meister's favorite words, *Raum*, appears not just to refer to the concept of space in itself, but to the actual "room" in the villa at Wannsee where the "devastation, gigantic" of the Holocaust was first set in motion. "Things," in this context, do not just "happen punctually / in space" but, rather, *take their course punctually in the room* where "the powers" make this decision. We point to this alternate reading here, though we have chosen not to be guided by Meister's marginalia in rendering the poem into English. While our version thus remains, as it is in the German, fairly abstract, we nonetheless hope that the poem's possible political context will shine a useful and unsettling light on Meister's signature existential obsessions.

However gnomic his poems may at times be, Meister resolutely rejects the postwar notion that the Holocaust is unrepresentable and that it may have even dealt a fatal blow to poetic language as such. In his personal correspondence he writes, "Auschwitz does not necessarily have to cripple language . . . On the contrary, language can't help but lift up reality (which does not mean it poeticizes it); otherwise reality remains pebbles upon pebbles." Meister's comparison of a languageless reality to stony sediment echoes Paul Celan's Bremen address—a copy of which Celan mailed to Meister several years earlier following their meeting in Paris—in which Celan uses the word *angereichert* (enriched), a word we often associate with soil (and one that contains *Reich*, a possible reason for Celan's scare quotes):

> It, the language, remained, not lost, yes in spite of everything. But it had to pass through its own answerlessness, pass through frightful muting, pass through the thousand darknesses of deathbringing speech. It passed through and gave back no words for that which happened; yet it passed through this happening. Passed through and could come to light again, "enriched" by all this. (Felstiner translation)

By way of their verse, poets such as Meister and Celan affirm language's efficacy, emphasizing its indispensable powers of adaptation and survival. They thus refuse to accept Theodor Adorno's oft-quoted (but all too often decontextualized and misunderstood) dictum that "to write poetry after Auschwitz is barbaric," and they reject the notion that language must necessarily remain bankrupt in the wake of atrocity. Like Celan, who waits for language to "pass through" its failures and renew itself, Meister manages a strangely patient faith in poetic speech. "I never found myself in flight from the sentence," he writes in a programmatic note to this volume. To relinquish the sentence, he says, "is a vanity of those who adorn themselves with having discovered its impotence."

These statements may seem strange coming from the author of verse that so frequently challenges its reader's understanding. Meister is nonetheless clear about the limits of his expression, though he repeatedly insists on the productivity of being able to trace their contours. Unlike those who he says proclaim language's supposed impotence, Meister does not relish negativity as means or end in his poems; rather, he celebrates language's ability to reveal reality for what it is: that which escapes unitary representation. This power Meister calls a "negative positivity": "Of course my efforts to formulate the sentence with the aim of totality could only expose and thus declare the breach of unity—this is a kind of negative positivity."

It is in this context that the title of this volume must be understood. The imperative is not to "say the sentence *about* entirety"—there is no such unit of meaning that contains the whole of everything. (*Satz*, we should note, can denote either "sentence" or "proposition.") It would be hubris to assume language were capable of saying—and thus somehow containing—this "totality." The imperative of the title, rather, is to say something *having to do with* this whole, something that "entirety" contains—not the other way around. The "sentence" is only one such thing contained within the whole (the others can be found listed in the poem on page 89 that begins with the title's five words: "the break, / the cleft clamor, the / torpid tone, the days' / light"). The book's self-reflexive call to "say the sentence" that is "of entirety" is thus a poetic charge to seize upon language as a vital and necessary part of a totality that must exceed representation, a part (or "break" or "rift") of a whole that exposes that whole as illusory. In Meister's play of words, it is a "myth," the other meaning of the word *Sage*—what seems to be "entirety" is really only a "breach of unity." Language, then, does not fail to represent this totality; rather, it succeeds as the index of a reality that is only available to us in fragments. In this, Meister echoes Adorno's assertion that "the whole [das Ganze] is the false."

If for Meister language can only succeed by conveying a ruptured totality, then it would seem all the more apparent that, as we stated at the close of our introduction to *In Time's Rift*, translation from one language to another must be in some sense impossible. This is not at all to say that the activity isn't useful or pleasurable or necessary, but only to say that it is often extremely difficult to transform a reading experience in one language into a reading experience in another without sometimes changing the very essence of the original. Basic communication is one thing—every language has a way in which one might formulate a clear request for a glass of water or directions to the restroom—but trying to replicate the sonic, visual, and syntactical elements of the source text in a translation can at times be futile, which in turn proves very frustrating to those of us who acknowledge that such elements are never beside the point to the poet.

Several poems in this volume proved difficult in this way, a notable example being "Kind Keiner" (on page 20), which contains visual and sonic wordplay in German that simply cannot be fully rendered into English. The final word of the second stanza (*Seine*) of course refers to the river in which Paul Celan drowned, a word that is also, however, a homograph of the German word for "his." Were Meister to have intended the German nominalized possessive pronoun instead of the French river, then *Seine* would have rhymed with *Meine*, which appears at the end of the first two lines of the next stanza and also in *Allgemeine* (the universal) in the fourth line. Though their last three letters are indeed the same, "Seine" and "mine" still lack the extreme visual similarity and the pronominal kinship of *Seine* and *Meine*, a loss for which our rhyming of "mine" and "consigned"—an attempt to echo the *Meine/Allgemeine* rhyme—does not make up. (It's worth noting that interlingual wordplay is also discernible in *Allgemeine*, which looks very similar to *Allemagne*, the French word for Germany, as well as in *je* (ever), which, as David Wellbery has pointed out, can also be read as the French first-person pronoun.) The stanza concludes with three lines that end with the same syllable—the *-ben* in *Sterben, Leben*, and *gegeben*—and while we've managed to replicate this with the syllable "-ing," our rendering lacks the punch of Meister's original, in that his close rhyming of *Leben* and *gegeben* prepares the reader for the poem's conclusion far more forcefully than our "dying" and "living."

Our translation of this poem's final stanza ("Because some / things rhyme.") refers to the very qualities of the original poem we've had to erase or diminish, which in turn doesn't make adequately evident the simultaneous affinity for and distance from Celan that Meister is trying to conjure. Instances such as this one make us all the more grateful to Wave Books for agreeing to print the original poems alongside our renderings.

Lastly, we offer a brief heads-up to those readers who may be used to our previous translations, in which each poem occupies its own page: In this volume, the poem on page 40 extends to a second page.

GRAHAM FOUST AND SAMUEL FREDERICK

Sage vom Ganzen
den Satz, den Bruch,
das geteilte Gewölbe, den
trägen Ton, die Tage
Lieds.
Mühsam
im gestimmten Raum
die Zeit in den Körpern,
leidiges Geheimnis, langsam,
Tod immer.

(Und ich wollt doch
da Auge nicht missen
erstehung der faserlosen nah um.)

Sage: DIES ist kein anderes.
Sage: so fiel, in gemeiner Verwirrung,
der Fall. Sage auch immer:
die Erfindung war groß.

Da darfst nur mich
Liebe verraten.

                    Ernst Meister

Der Mensch

hat sein Lied zu singen,

und bin ich auch

gerüttelt von der Weltstille,

ich will nichts werfen

über seinen Scheitel.

Mankind
has his song to sing,
and even though I am
shaken by the world's silence,
I don't want to fling anything
over the crown of his head.

I

Noch zu
erzählen, noch zu
erzählen . . . mein
Gedächtnis
fragt mich, und ich
starre es an.

Leb ich?
frag ich mein Zimmer,—
frag ich
den Raum in der Weite
und schließlich:
Bist du, Raum,
was ich weiß?

Still to
tell, still to
tell . . . my
memory
asks me, and I
stare at it.

Am I alive?
I ask my room,—
I ask
the space in the expanse
and lastly:
Are you, space,
what I know?

Er ist, der Leib,
in seiner Arbeit
kein Traum
und ein Traum.

Blick ihn an,
den Fremdling,
damit du
ihn hieltest

und hättest,
einen Nächsten,
nah dem Bodenlosen
hier.

In its labor
the body is
no dream
and a dream.

Look at it,
the stranger,
so that you
might hold it

and have it,
someone near,
close to what is bottomless
here.

Wenn wir
entblößt sind
bis auf den
Lehm, dann
ist die Rede
richtig vom
Sangbaren.

Zu Ende gedacht
den geborenen Menschen,
tönt's zurück.

When we're
stripped right
down to
clay, then
the talk of
what's singable
is right.

The man who is born,
thought through to the end—
it echoes back.

Viele
haben keine Sprache.

Wär ich nicht selbst
satt von Elend, ich

bewegte
die Zunge nicht.

Many
have no language.

Were I not myself
replete with misery, I

would not
move my tongue.

Es schlug einer,
ein Lehrer,
mit dem Stock auf den Tisch:

Zu sterben, das ist
Grammatik!

Ich lachte.

Nimm den Leib
wörtlich, das Wort
leiblich.

Ich lachte.

Ich starb.

für Gregor Laschen

Someone,
a teacher,
hit the desk with a stick:

To die, that is
grammar!

I laughed.

Take the body
literally, the word
bodily.

I laughed.

I died.

for Gregor Laschen

Sie schlummern,
die Väter, die Brüder.

Im Hohlen wanderst du
ihrer Schädel und hörst.

Kommt doch von weit
Gedicht und Gedanke,

der Schwersinn,
die Arbeit.

They slumber,
the fathers, the brothers.

You wander in the hollow
of their skulls and hear.

Yet from afar comes
poem and thought,

the melancholy,
the labor.

II

Sieh an
im gekrümmten Spiegel
das O,
die Ellipse,
darin eines Sterns
seufzerloser Versuch
mit Tier- und
Menschengestalt.

Alles
ist jung, alles
entsetzlich alt.

Behold
in the bent mirror
the O,
the ellipse,
therein a star's
sighless experiment
with animal and
human shape.

All of it
is young, all of it
terribly old.

Das zu
Erfahrende, das zu
Verhandelnde heißt
ICH und ist
beim Messen des Menschen
ein Beispiel,
über dem selben Versuch
von Toten gebaut.

What's there
to experience, what's there
to negotiate is called
I and is
by the measure of mankind
an example,
built over the same endeavor
of the dead.

Kind keiner
Jahreszeit,
sondern des wittrigen
Rätsels von je . . .

Sommer . . . gegönnter . . .
So dieser, überm
Gottesgerippe flammender
oder der schmierigen
Seine.

Das Meine
ist als das Meine
ungequält
ans Allgemeine, ihr Nachbarn,
unser Leben und Sterben,
Sterben und Leben
gegeben.

Denn manches
reimt sich.

Child of no
season,
but of the inclement
riddle of ever . . .

Summer . . . bestowed . . .
So this one, over
God's skeleton flaming
or of the smeary
Seine.

What's mine
is as what's mine
consigned,
untormented,
to the universal, you neighbors,
our living and dying
dying and living.

Because some
things rhyme.

Demnach, nach-
denklich, Tier
in der Wildnis . . .
Gerücht der
eigenen Spur . . .
einsam im
seltsamen Jahr.

Es steht
ein Turm, Turm
an einem Fluß.
Der murmelt
menschlich, er
stammelt.
Dort

sprang es vorbei.

Thus, thought-
fully, creature
in the wilderness . . .
whisper of
its own trail . . .
alone in the
peculiar year.

A tower, tower
standing
by a river.
Which murmurs
humanly, it
stammers.
That's where

it sprang past.

Kern der Erde,
die Glut,
sah ich vom Wasser,
der strömenden
Fläche gespiegelt.

Und von oben
der Stern trat,
Pol zu Pol,
in die Mitte
nüchternen Feuers.

Earth's core,
the glow,
I saw it in the water,
mirrored in
the streaming surface.

And from on high
the star stepped,
pole to pole,
into the center
of sober fire.

(Die Flüsse allerdings
von niemand,
das Meer noch minder
je auszutrinken)

Geborgen. Kein
fetter Mann, gern
essend in Frankreich, sondern
sein Fleisch
gesättigt mit Wasser, Aas,
weiß blühend, Algen
zur einen Rose, der
»Wahrheit selbst«.

(The rivers, however,
not ever to be drunk up—
the oceans even less—
by anyone)

Salvaged. No
fat man, savoring
a meal in France, rather
his flesh
sated with water, carcass,
blooming white, algae
into the one rose, into
"truth itself."

Wer denn hat diesen
von brüchigen Stegen
gesprungenen Menschen
gefischt, den dieser
Wortzeit?

Du, ich, ohne
Netz, Sichel, Haken,
du und
ich mit vier
nackten Händen,

ICH, DU, die
Unbekannten?

Einer wars, einer
am Kai, Spieler
mit bilderlosen Karten.

Keiner.

Who then fished this
person who jumped
from moldering walkways
—him of this
wordtime?

You, I, without
net, sickle, hook,
you and
I with four
naked hands,

I, YOU, the
unknown ones?

It was someone, someone
on the quay, a player
with faceless cards.

No one.

Preisgegeben,
ein Turm,
gilb,
schief vor Trauer.

Kann nicht
beiseite tun
im Schreiten, lächerlich,
Herbstlaub.

Kann
überhaupt
nicht gehn,

steht da beim
spiegelnden Flusse
wie aufrecht.

Abandoned,
a tower,
yellowed,
crooked with grief.

Cannot
push aside,
midstride, ridiculous,
autumn's leaves.

Can't
even go
at all,

stands there by
the reflecting river
as if upright.

Den Atem ausgetauscht
wirklich.
Jetzt, schönes Nun,
die Luft steht still.

Verlassen nicht
und nicht versäumen.
Was Beteuerung war,
Geräusch der Öde.

Ich hab dir
das Meine
umsonst gesagt,

und so rede
ein Jedes
das Seine umsonst.

Breath traded out
really.
Now, lovely moment,
the air stands still.

Not to abandon
and not to forsake.
What assurance was,
sound of the wasteland.

In vain
I told you
what's mine,

and so may each
speak its own
in vain.

Da keineswegs
bei dir
das Meer das letzte Wort hat

(sondern von nun
das Trockene
dir zum Trank dient),

so müßt ich
deinen Namen tilgen
am Grund des Sees.

Das aber
kann ich nicht . . .

Ich bleibe
dort beim Grund
mit deinen Augen,

gesunkenem Gebein
und Zeug
der Oberwelt.

Because in no way
with you
does the ocean have the last word

(rather, from now on
dry land
will serve as your drink),

I would need to
erase your name
at the bottom of the sea.

But I
can't do that . . .

I'll stay
there by the bottom
with your eyes,

your sunken bones
and stuff
from the world above.

Wenn uns noch einmal
Augen gegeben würden
nach mancher Zeit
in der Leiche, dem Tode . . .

Als wir uns liebten,
betrachtetest du
sehr genau
meinen Schädel.

If we would once again
be given eyes
after some time
in the corpse, in death . . .

As we made love,
you examined
my cranium
very closely.

(Die Not, sie
wendet sich
mit ihrem
Altertumsgesicht
und sieht sich um
nach Jahr und Tag)

Ob ich auch
hänge
an deinem Haar:

so verhallend
wie möglich
rufe ich dich

tief in der Zeit
des sich weigernden Echos,
der menschenlosen.

Genau in dem Zufall
hör ich dich sagen:
Ich lieb dich nicht mehr.

(Misery, it
turns
with its
ancient face
and looks about
for year and day)

Whether I too
hang
on your hair:

trailing off as much
as possible,
I call you

deep in the time
of the echo that refuses,
the humanless time.

At that chance moment
I hear you say:
I don't love you anymore.

Hör's, wo ich weiß:
das Ich muß verlieren,
weil nämlich

der Äther, bewußtlos,
der Gott ist
von allem.

I hear it, where I know:
the I has to lose,
precisely because

the ether, unconscious,
is the god
of everything.

(Vorm roten Sonnball
wird Verstand
sich vorsehn,
doch Zauber
nicht verschmähn
zulieb dem Toren)

Als ob ich nicht wüßte
im Blitze, den du
erinnerst der Nacht,

mir sind grau,
genau in die Schläfen
die Zeichen gestochen.

Drum nimm
vorlieb oder
lieb mich deswegen,

jetzt, wo der jetzige
Sommer scharrt,
das schöne Skelett.

(Reason will
beware
the red ball of sun,
yet not forswear
magic
for the sake of the fool)

As if I didn't know
in the lightning, which you
recall from the night,

the signs
are pierced gray,
way into my temples.

Therefore
make do or
do love me for that,

currently, where the current
summer scrapes,
the shapely skeleton.

Du hörst mir zu,
ich hör dir zu.

Zu leben und
zu lieben die Dinge

(ein Satz von dir), wie
soll das gehn?

Man hat wohl Liebe
genug. Doch

keinem Leide, das
vollkommen Leid ist,

und keinem Tode
helf ich auf.

You listen to me,
I listen to you.

To live and
to love things

(a saying of yours), how
should that go?

It seems we have love
enough. But

I will help up
no grief that is grief

completely
and no death.

Liebesgedanken
abwärts
bis ins Tote
der Geschaffenheit,
das Mütterorakel
ratlos.

Lied
meiner Lieder:
einzige Gegenwart,
vom Nichts
sinnreich ausgespien.

Ziemlich ein Gott,
die—wörtlich—
weibliche Leere.

Thoughts of love
all the way down
to what's dead
of createdness,
the oracle of mothers
bewildered.

Song
of my songs:
only presence,
spewed from
nothingness, ingeniously.

Quite a god,
the—literally—
feminine void.

IV

Sein, verfluchtes,

hat vom Schönen

oft das Gesicht, und

tausendmal schöner als

die hinter den Zeitbergen

unaufweckbar träumenden

Götter—so Aphrodite—

ein Liebliches von hier,

das vorbeikommt,

in sich vorübergeht, auch

alternd im täglichen Tal,

wo die Mühlen mahlen

von fern des Meers.

Being, accursed,
from beauty
it gets its face, and

a thousand times more beautiful than
those unwakeable dreamers
behind the mountains of time,

the gods—Aphrodite, say—
a lovely one from hereabouts,

that comes around,
that passes by in itself, even

growing old in the everyday vale,
where the mills mill
far from the ocean.

Der Blitz
ist von eigener Hand
und entzündet
dein Haar.

Es komme
Feuersbrunst,
wo das Dach birst,
der Boden reißt.

Komm,
ein Frieren kommt,
das brennendste.

The bolt
is from my own hand
and ignites
your hair.

Let it come,
a conflagration,
where the roof bursts,
the ground rips.

Come,
a freezing is coming,
the most blazing.

Langsame Zeit,
Zeitlangsamkeit,
Wortlangsamkeit,
langsam, ich sage
ein Zeitwort,
ich sage es dir
zum Vertraun,
es ist
Sterben darin,
Mond und Sonne,
die Glut,
die Häuser anzündet,
Glocken auch,
daß sie schimmern.

Ein Jahr
ist kein Glück,
die Toten
sind keine Helfer.
Darum
komme von deiner Seite
mir der Bescheid
irgendwie, wie
es weitergeh
und so weiter
zuletzt.

Slow time,
time slowness,
word slowness,
slowly, I say
a verb, time's word,
I say it to you
for trust,
there is
dying in it,
moon and sun,
the blaze
that ignites houses,
bells too,
so that they shimmer.

A year
is no bliss,
the dead
won't lend you a hand.
Therefore
let me hear from your side
confirmation
somehow, how
it may go on
and so on
in the end.   **57**

Nahes, die Nähe,

das rasche und volle

Erkennen, das gern

ins Schwierige rückt

und Augen des Lebens macht.

Heiser werden die Glocken,

wenn eine Gegenwart

der Zukunft wegen,

verläßlich gewähnter,

beiseitegeht.

Something near, nearness,
the quick and complete
recognition, which likes
to edge into difficulty
and makes life eyes.

The bells become hoarse,
when on account of the future,
assumed reliable,
a present moment
steps aside.

Zeit, Zeit . . .
Winter ein Winter . . .
Haben die Toten es gut?

Gerade noch
aus purpurnem Eise
hat mich angeblickt

Leben,
Haar hinunter die Wange,
bang gewendet.

Time, time . . .
Winter a winter . . .
Do the dead have it good?

Just in time
from out of crimson ice
I was looked at

by life,
hair down the cheek,
turned anxiously.

Schau in die Handfläche.
Immerzu
scheint Abschied auf.

Ein Ton wohnt bei
und endet nicht
gegen die Hügelränder.

Look into the opened hand.
Departure
keeps showing up there.

A sound is present
and doesn't end
against the edges of the hills.

V

Eingemauert ein Schiff.
Im gescheiterten Leibe
Schlaf.

Die Segel
hören nicht auf,
weiß zu sein,

ob auch Knechte, grau,
der Notwendigkeit Schüler,
die Wächter sind.

Walled in, a ship.
In the dashed body
sleep.

The sails
do not cease
being white,

even when servants, gray,
necessity's pupils,
are standing guard.

IN SÈTE

Den Stein verstand ich,
der die Namen trug,
ihn waagrecht, sein Gewicht.

Die Schädel drunten
dacht ich so: es wäre
Lehm daraus zu löffeln.

Bewußtsein, überlebt
vom Stoff.

Ich war

der Atmende, aufrechtes
Tier auf Erden noch—
im Weltriß häuslich.

IN SÈTE

I understood the stone
that carried the names,
its levelness, its weight.

The skulls below,
I think them thus: one
might spoon out clay.

Consciousness, outlived
by substance.
I was

the one breathing, upright
creature still on Earth—
at home in the rip of the world.

O Stillstand
wie ein Grab.
Es schleudert Gischt das Meer
in diese Bucht.
Die Hand
vom Wirklichen geführt:
die lange Kunst gesponnen.
Der pünktliche Gedanke
fällt mit dem Strich
des Horizonts zusammen.

Spät ists.

O stagnation
like a grave.
The sea sloshes foam
into this bay.
The hand
guided by what's real:
the long art spun.
The punctual thought
and the line of
the horizon coincide.

It's late.

Schönste Dame,
längst alt
und sehr ängstlich,
wart nur, es sänftigt
sich alles, wenn bald
mein Gerippe
der frömmste Sohn ist
von deinem.

Von dir
weiß eines
die Sekunde sehr genau,
lacht
deines Ungeschicks . . . es kommt

das Namenlos, wo dir auch
Tod, der Ton, entklingt,
wo dann das Licht
mit Julikirschen geht,
des Himmels Würgen kommt.

Ach, daß ihr alle,
schon gestorben, mir vergebt,
wenn sich die Angst gebiert,
das dir bis jetzt
nur halb bekannte Kind.

Most beautiful lady,
long aged
and very afraid,
just wait, all will
be assuaged, when soon
my skeleton
is the most pious son
of *yours.*

Of you
the instant knows
one thing very well,
laughs
at your awkwardness . . . the

Nameless is coming, when even
death, its tone, will ring from you;
when light goes away
with the cherries of July;
the heavens come choking.

Oh, may all of you,
already dead, forgive me,
when fright births itself
the child that is only
half-known to you.   **73**

(Es bleibt
eine Höhle,
gesichtslos wie klanglos)

Entschlafen, ent-
träumt,
nicht einmal
ein Halm.

Denk es,
und zur Kugel
nimm dich
zusammen.

Die meisten
Sterne
sind leblos.

(There remains
a cave,
as faceless as silent)

Passed away asleep, a-
dream,
not even
a blade of grass.

Think it,
and pull
yourself
into a ball.

Most
stars
are lifeless.

VI

Menschen, wenn sie
leben, sind
empfindliche Särge.

Was mehr
konnte es geben als
solche Blüte
im Nichts, das ein Nichts
nicht sein kann, vielmehr,
stofflich, ein Begehrendes ist.

Warte dich ab
als aus dem Wasser,
der Wiege Orakeltes
anderes Nichts.

Humans, when they're
alive, are
sensitive coffins.

What more
could there have been than
such blossoming
in nothingness, which cannot
be a nothing, but is much more,
tangibly, something desired.

Await yourself
as that which was augured,
from water, the cradle—
another nothing.

Die Be-
fangenheit und
Gefangenheit, wie sie, die
Zeit, listige Totschlägerin,
Schleifen macht,
mit langer Weile
um ein Leben sich dreht—
doch das ist

nur wenig an Schmerz,
anderes gibts, woran
das schwerste Lot hängt
der Erde. Neulich wieder
das Kind, den Krüppel der Sinne
gesehn.

Em-
barrassment and
imprisonment, how it,
time, cunning murderess,
makes loops,
orbiting one lifetime
in dull intervals—
but that is

only a little of pain,
there's something else, from which
Earth's heaviest plummet
hangs. Recently saw
the child, the cripple of the senses
again.

Weisheit, müßige Weise,
mag auch ein Schnitt gehn
scharf durch Augen.

Nicht können
die ganze Liebe und Schuld, das
ganze Entsetzen.

Auch Schämen nicht immer,
so an Tagen, die
schmecken.

Wisdom, the idle wise,
might even a cut go
sharply across the eyes.

Unable—
all that love and guilt, all
that horror.

Also never to be ashamed,
as on days that
taste good.

Der neben mir
wirft die Glieder,
der neben mir ringt
wie nach Atem um Sprache,
und ich seh meinen Bruder
vom Leben getrennt.

Der Mensch
hat sein Lied zu singen,
und bin ich auch
gerüttelt von der Weltstille,
ich will nichts werfen
über seinen Scheitel.

The man beside me
flings his limbs;
the man beside me struggles
for speech as if for breath,
and I see my brother
cut off from life.

Mankind
has his song to sing,
and even though I am
shaken by the world's silence,
I don't want to fling anything
over the crown of his head.

Sitzen im eigenen
Haus, bei Fenstern
schwachäugig.—Zu ermessen
des Menschen Elle
ist traurig, aber
sie wollen doch wohnen.

Wars gestern, da
hast du von jungen Tänzern gehört,
die verbrannten,
Liebliche nie gesehen,
behältst du das?

Wenn es im Erdkreis,
ja, wie du willst,
vor der Haustür, gräßlich
gibt, wen grauts?

Über den Begriff
geht mir
des Ganzen Trost.

Sitting in one's own
house, near windows,
weak-eyed.—To measure
the human cubit
is sad, but
they still want to dwell.

Was it yesterday, when
you heard of young dancers,
who burned up,
lovelies never seen,
will you hold on to that?

If in this world,
sure, have it your way,
here at the front door, horror's
there, who's horrified?

I'm baffled
by the solace
of entirety.

Sage vom Ganzen
den Satz, den Bruch,
das geteilte Geschrei, den
trägen Ton, der Tage
Licht.

Mühsam
im gestimmten Raum
die Zeit in den Körpern,
leidiges Geheimnis, langsam.
Tod immer.

(Und ich wollt doch
das Auge nicht missen
entlang den Geschlechtern nach uns.)

Sage: DIES ist kein anderes.
Sage: So fiel, in gemeiner Verwirrung,
der Fall. Sage auch immer:
Die Erfindung war groß.

Du darfst nur nicht
Liebe verraten.

Of entirety say
the sentence, the break,
the cleft clamor, the
torpid tone, the days'
light.

Arduously
in the attuned space
time in the bodies,
exasperating secret, slowly.
Death always.

(And I didn't want
to do without the eye
along the generations after us.)

Say: THIS is none other.
Say: Thus fell, in common bafflement,
the Fall. And say always:
The invention was vast.

Just don't go
and betray love.

VII

Rose—
sie selber
stachelt nichts.

Uns stichts,
wir schliefen denn,
entfernt vom Widerspruch.

Nichts
sticht den Raum.
Ach,

anders er
(und unverborgen)
als unser

wie Nüsse klüglich
eingeschaltes
Hirn.

Es schreit.

Rose—
it alone
sticks nothing.

It pricks us,
for we would sleep,
removed from contradiction.

Nothing
pricks the space.
Ah,

that's different
(and unconcealed)
from our

wisely shelled-in
and nutlike
brain.

It screams.

Pünktlich gehts zu
im Raum
gemäß den Kräften
außen und innen.
Zur Stunde wieder
Verheerung, gigantisch.

Die schwer eingeborene
Schwäche, was
gewahrt sie denn wirklich?

Das Sehn
will nicht wissen,
und wenig gilt
heute und morgen
der Jammer.

Things happen punctually
in space,
as per the powers
outside and inside.
On the hour, again,
devastation, gigantic.

The profoundly inborn
weakness, what
does it even notice?

Seeing
doesn't want to know,
and the wailing
today and tomorrow
counts for little.

Selbst unterm
entzauberten Mond
reden die Mütter
den Kindern nicht wahr,
und am Tage hör ich
der Alten Geschwätz.

Die im Schaden umhergehn
und stolpern, wir alle,
sind auch im Tode
nicht ärmer als jetzt.

Even under the
disenchanted moon
mothers do not speak
the truth to their children,
and during the day I hear
the chatter of the elders.

Those who wander in damage
and stumble, all of us,
are also not any poorer
in death than now.

Am Ende der Tage,
was kommt
für ein Gestotter aus
des Menschen Mund,

wenn die Schwierigkeit
zum Krüppel wird
allüberhaupt
und Kälte der Himmel
zufriert die Akte.

Sprache vormals,
diese Liebschaft,
als schon das Lied
den Kopf verlor.

At the end of days,
what kind
of stammering will come
from mankind's mouth,

when difficulty
becomes a cripple,
if anything at all,
and the heavens' coldness
freezes the acts over.

Language formerly,
this romance,
when the song already
lost its head.

Dereinst,
wenn die Letzten
sich guttun
über dem Aschegehäuf,

die Liebe
die blindeste ist
seit den Zeiten, wo die,
die selber vergaßen,
Kinder der Unzeit,
vergessen sind durchaus . . .

wir—ihr im
unaufhörbaren
sternigen
Unglück.

Someday,
when the last ones
are doing well for themselves
above the ashheap,

when love
is the most blind
since the times, when those
who themselves forgot,
children of untime,
are completely forgotten . . .

we—you all
in the unstoppable
starry
misfortune.

Das war
gemacht, um
da zu sein
und zu verschwinden.

Der Schlange Zunge
hat in dem Spalt
von Tag und Nacht
gefunkelt.

Genug. Die
einzige Ewigkeit
verbracht.

Genug, vorbei

Unsinn und Sinn
der Sinne.

This was
made to
be there
and to disappear.

In the rift
of day and night
the snake's tongue
sparkled.

Enough. The
only eternity
spent.
Enough, past

nonsense and sense
of the senses.

Alles scheint Rand
trotz (»unendlich«)
der Tiefe,
an dem sich Verwesung
wie Schimmel ansetzt.

Mir graut.

Im Hirne
erscheinend die Wimpern
ganz weiß
und vor den Augen
unköniglich Purpur.

In der Gegend
zu hören
ein Lied ohne Ton.

Everything seems edge
despite ("endless")
the depth,
to which rot
grows like mildew.

I'm horrified.

Appearing in the brain
the eyelashes
all white
and before the eyes
unroyal purple.

To hear
nearby
a song without sound.

In Stücken seines
Begriffs,
vom Schleim umwunden
der Zeitschlange,
todestöricht der Mensch.

Im Jedermannsland,
im Viereck auf Papier
tun sich täglich
Namen davon.

Was du selber
lebst, gib acht,
schon vergangen.

In pieces of their
concepts,
wound up with the slime
of time's snake,
humans are death-daft.

In everyman's-land,
in a square on paper
names daily
make themselves scarce.

What you yourself
live, pay mind,
already passed.

Nicht vom
Planeten, dem Vater,
nicht von dessen
Vater, dem Raum,
der Abgrund,

sondern wir
gähnen ihn,
träge,
in der Angst,
verstörend einander.

Am schwersten
reichen die Menschen
ans Eigene,
allzu sterblich.

Not from
the planet, the father,
not from his
father, from space,
the abyss;

rather, we
yawn *it*—
sluggish,
in distress,
perturbing one another.

All too mortal,
people strain
the most to get
to their own.

Denk, in den
Jahrtrillionen
darfst du
kein Heimweh mehr haben
nach Mensch und Erde.

DIES, daß du
ein Kind warst
des Alls,
ist dahin,
und wo

ist die Unheilige,
die Mutter mit Sinnen
allsamt geblieben
und wo
das Gestirn, das uns schien?

Mir schwindelt.

Ich wünscht auch,
eh geendet, ich säh
einen Traum.

Think, in the
quintillionth year
you won't
be allowed to be homesick
for person and Earth.

THIS, that you
were a child
of the universe,
is gone,
and where

is the unholy one,
the mother with her
wits about her,
and where
the star that shone for us?

I'm reeling.

I also wished,
before it ended, I'd see
a dream.

Warum
ist das
eine Arbeit,
aus dem Nichts
zu gelangen
ins Nichts,
statt des leichtesten
Flügelsprungs?

Soll nichts
geschehn geradezu?

Warum
setz ich mich nicht
mit dem Mut der
unterbrechbaren Luft
auf deine
schreibende Hand?

Why
is it
exertion
to get from
nothingness
into nothingness,
instead of the easiest
winged leap?

Is nothing even
supposed to happen?

Why
do I not sit
with the courage of
interruptible air
on your
writing hand?

Hauptsächlich
Lebenspfade.

Mit den Binsen
geschwätzt und auf Schilf
Denken geschrieben.

Den Menschen
nicht verlassen,
ihn fürchtend auch.

Life's paths
primarily.

Chatted with the rushes
and wrote thinking
on the reeds.

Humanity—
not forsaken,
but also dreaded.

Geh nur immer
durch Häuser,
bleibe, wenn

kein Geschwätz ist
bei Menschen, weil sie
ihre Tage halbwegs
verstehn, nicht anders

als du, der—
einfältiges Bild—
den Boden der Grüfte
durchbricht,

um deutlich
hier zu sein.

Just keep going
through houses;
stay, if

there's no chatter
among people, since they
partway understand
their days, not unlike

you, who—
guileless image—
breaks through
the floor of the crypts,

so as to be
here, clearly.

Es ist
von Himmels wegen,
seiner Dehnung ohne Maß,
ein Geheiß, zu ehren
das Dingliche und es
tönen zu lassen
durch den Schmerz.

Bewimpert aber,
das Auge,
ist eine Liebe.

It is
by decree of the heavens,
by its extension without measure,
a call to honor
the thingly and to
let it resound
through pain.

Lashed, however,
the eye,
is a love.

Ich, Riff
im Mutterleibe
(noch keine
Woge ertönend)
sollte einst wissen:

Gezeugt, muß einer
zeugen das Licht
und die Finsternis
gleichso.

I, reef

in the womb

(no wave

yet resounding)

should one day know:

Begotten, someone must

beget the light

and the darkness

alike.

Die Fahrt
gegen die Sonne.

Der Augen Untergang
im Schlaglicht des Wahren.

Ein Drittes zweier Mitten
fällt aus der Zeit.

Schmerz, der Schatten,
verwaist.

The trip
toward the sun.

The demise of the eyes
in the hard light of the true.

A third from two midsts
drops out of time.

Pain, the shadow,
orphans.

Eine
Verbeugung noch, tänzerisch,
wie es einmal
der Brauch war,
und dann
nimm uns, schwarzes Licht,
auf in deine Wohnung.

Es ist
ein jedes
seiner nicht sicher.

Seid ihr es,
Sonnen?

Just one
more genuflection, dancelike,
as once was
the custom,
and then
receive us, black light,
into your dwelling.

Every
being is
uncertain of itself.

Are you,
suns?

Die hier im Wahrschein
bloß versprechliche,
die blinde Rose ...

Wir werden, du und ich,
geschlagen sein
von einer Sonne Tatze,

Sonne,
die wir sahn,—
warum?

Cur aliquid vidi?

Here in the seeming-true,
merely promiseful,
the blind rose . . .

We will, you and I,
be beaten
by one of the sun's paws,

sun,
which we've seen,—
why?

Cur aliquid vidi?

O
mein Grauen, die
Ellipse steht aufrecht
. . . ein Öhr.

Die andere Seite,
gesehnt, nicht da,
es erübrigt sich
der Versuch
für das Tragtier.

Ach, die
Augenblicke des Friedens
durchstoßen,
ein Loch
starrt dich an.

O
my horror, the
ellipse stands upright
. . . a needle's eye.

The other side,
longed for, not there,
there is no need
for the pack animal
to try.

Alas, the
moments of peace
pierced through,
a hole
stares at you.

Du, mein

schwerster Begriff,

Leichnam, Schädelton

noch—du lebst—und

tauber Schädel

unvergessender Nachton.

Behüte, Unbekannte,

mich sehr

während der Frist,

in der

meine Finger

mich zählen.

You, my
most difficult concept,
corpse, sound of skull
still—you're alive—and
deaf skull
unforgetting aftersound.

Unknown one, look after
me well
during the time

allotted
for my fingers
to count me.

Hier,

gekrümmt

zwischen zwei Nichtsen,

sage ich Liebe.

Hier, auf dem

Zufallskreisel

sage ich Liebe.

Hier, von den hohlen

Himmeln bedrängt,

an Halmen

des Erdreichs mich haltend,

hier, aus dem

Seufzer geboren,

von Abhang

und Abhang gezeugt,

sage ich Liebe.

Here,
doubled over
between two nothings,
I say love.
Here, on the
randomly spinning toy,
I say love.
Here, beset
by the hollow heavens,
holding tight to stems
of the soil,
here, birthed from
the sigh,
from cliff
and cliff begotten,
I say love.

Von allen Menschenwesen der Verbleib:
der Himmel ist nicht zärtlich.
Er ist Gesetz, ein
Wissen ohne Wissen.

Du hast bald deinen Tag dahingebracht
und läßt erst recht
das Zeitgeschwätz beiseit,
setzt aus Geduld die Zeile.

Aus einem Wort wie Leben
macht der Blitz ein Haus.
Ihm mangelt nicht die Tür.
Sie führt ins Offene.

The whereabouts of all human creatures:
the heavens are not gentle.
They are the law, a
knowledge without knowledge.

You've just about lived out your day
and only now let
the chatter of time aside,
set, with patience, the line of verse.

Out of a word like living
lightning makes a house.
It isn't lacking a door.
That leads into the open.

Und bis zuletzt
zärtliche Wissenschaft.
Das Vergebliche, kann sein,
nicht umsonst. Das
wirklich Nichtige aber
ist voll deutlich
immer da.

Es bleibt,
daß ich der Erde gehöre,
grausiger Mutter, in
geliebtesten Augen dunkelnd,
gehöre dem männlichen
Gestirn, ein

Same des Zufalls,
von des Äthers
Neugier gekauft.

And to the end
gentle science.
What's futile—could be—
not in vain. But
what's null and void
is completely obviously
always there.

It remains
that I belong to the earth,
ghastly mother, darkening
in most beloved eyes;
belong to the male
star, a

seed of chance,
bought by the curiosity
of the ether.

Fleisch, mein Wort,
einverleibend zeit-
kindlichen Spott,
Körper, bald

selbstvergessen im
Grabgeruch, während
der Äther
ohne Begierde herrscht.

Gott, dieser Gott:
der gehöhlteste Name
streicht sich,
vielkönnend, durch.

Flesh, my word,
incorporating time-
childlike mockery,
body, soon

oblivious in
the sepulchral smell, while
the ether
rules without desire.

God, this God:
the most hollow name
strikes itself,
able all around, out.

Totenreich, darin
Lebendiges sich träumt.
Es scheint, ich sehe,
ich sehe Schein,
Kadaverspur dazwischen.

Ist jetzt ein Nachmittag,
ist Sommer, das
Schwitzen vom Geschlecht?
In Schwebe der Geruch
der täglichen Geschichten.
So viel Mord.

Ohne Vernehmen ihrer selbst und
ohne unser Gespür
drehn sich die Sterne.
O fürchterliche Macht
der großen Körper.

Netherworld, in which
what's alive dreams itself.
It appears I see,
I see appearance,
trace of cadaver in between.

Is it now an afternoon,
is it summer, the
sweating from sex?
Suspended, the smell
of daily stories.
So much murder.

Without hearing themselves and
without our sensing,
the stars rotate.
O dreadful power
of great bodies.

XI

(».. . daß im Finstern für uns
einiges Haltbare sei«)

Vergessen, den Göttern
zu danken? Sie
mußt ich vergessen
und sollt noch vergessen
Fleisch und Blut und den
Wein einer Hochzeit.

Das kommt
aus dem Totenreich,
das es nicht gibt.

Das kommt
von dir, Todesmenschliche,
die es gibt.

("... that in the dark there may for us
be things that endure")

Forgetting—are the gods
to thank? It is they
I had to forget
and should still forget
flesh and blood and the
wine of a wedding.

That comes
from the netherworld,
which does not exist.

That comes
from you, grim reaper girl herself,
who does exist.

Getötet
von sich selbst, im Tode
leider auch entrückt
der einzigen Gewalt,
die Liebe hieß.

Niemand begreift
dies Lösliche,
es sei denn, er verstünde
die ganze List.

Dies ist ein Lied.

Killed
by his own hand; in death
alas, removed as well
from the only violence
that was called love.

No one will grasp
this soluble thing,
unless he were to understand
the whole ruse.

This is a song.

Dies ist ein Lied,
ein in das Hierige
getauchter Ring,
sein Gold
zerfallend freilich
immerzu.

Es ist
der deine, mit seinem
Steingefunkel anverwandelt
meiner Hand.
Ich laß ihn
trinken.

This is a song,
a ring dipped
into the here,
its gold
crumbling away, of course,
constantly.

It is
yours, with its
glistening stone adapted
to my hand.
I let it
drink.

Im Schlaf und

in Schluchten des Schlafs,

wenn du der Einen begegnest,

die sich nach Lüsten

zu erkennen gibt

als die Tote

mit schlagendem Herzen,

als die Mittlere

des gemilchten Raums

voll Gelächter der Knie

und der Schenkel,

und dich wirft alsbald

ins Labyrinth

begreifbaren Traums.

In sleep and
in chasms of sleep,
when you meet the one
who through her lusts
reveals herself
as the dead woman
with a beating heart,
as the mediator
of milky space
full of the laughter of knees
and of thighs,
and who flings you at once
into the labyrinth
of tangible dreams.

An jene Wand gelehnt,

das Verlies

(unsinnig fabeln muß ich,

als wär ich nicht augenlos),

heller Tag

des Fehlens der Sinne,

nicht all das Aas

schmeck ich, nicht

riech ich, Nichtin,

Fürstin hinter den Klippen,

deinen Blumenduft . . .

Während auch Jugend kommt

unter den Vielverschiedenen,

ein Mädchen jetzt . . .

Propped against that wall,
the dungeon
(I have to tell absurd tales
as if I weren't eyeless),
bright day
of the absence of senses,
I can't taste all
the carrion, nor
can I smell, Nothingess,
princess behind the cliffs,
your flower scent . . .

While even youth consorts
with those vastly different,
a girl now . . .

Die Worte sind fertig.
Umwunden von deinem Haar
ein jedes.

Dem ist
kein Räuber gewaltig,
wenn schon
die Sinne vergehen
beiden.

Nicht zu
vernichten ist
die Erscheinung.

The words are ready.
Each one wound up with
your hair.

Which
no robber can plunder,
even if
the meanings vanish
from both.

Not to be
annihilated,
the appearance.

Orakel geht
hindurch,
das Ende
spiegelt den Anfang.

Also hätte
ein Spiegel
zwei sehende
Seiten.

Im Schnittpunkt
der Augenblicke
wird das Rätsel
gesichtig.

für I. D.

Oracle goes
through,
the end
mirrors the beginning.

Thus a mirror
would have
two seeing
sides.

At the intersection
of these moments' glances
the riddle's face
will appear.

for I. D.

OUR WORK ON THESE TRANSLATIONS WAS
PARTLY FUNDED BY THE UNIVERSITY OF
DENVER. WE WOULD LIKE TO THANK LEA
PAO AND STEPHANIE JORDANS FOR THEIR
GENEROUS FEEDBACK ON MANY EARLY
DRAFTS OF THESE POEMS AND ALEXANDER
MOYSAENKO, BRITTANY DENNISON, HEIDI
BROADHEAD, AND JOSHUA BECKMAN AT
WAVE BOOKS FOR SEEING US THROUGH THE
FINAL STAGES OF ALL THREE VOLUMES.

THANK YOU DAVID CALIGIURI FOR THE
RIGHTING OF OUR MANY WRONGS.

LASTLY, WE WISH TO THANK REINHARD
MEISTER FOR GIVING US PERMISSION TO
REPRODUCE THE FACSIMILE OF THE POEM
FROM WHICH THIS VOLUME TAKES ITS TITLE.